A Taste of Cranberries and some tales too...

Phoebe's Kitchen™

Written and Edited by
P. Ann Pieroway

Cover and Illustrations by
Rafael Perez

Designed by
Gianna M. Perez

Bass Pond
P R E S S
Springfield, MA

A Taste of Cranberries and some tales too...

Published by
Bass Pond Press
P O Box 6, East Longmeadow, MA 01028, U.S.A.
info@basspondpress.com

Library of Congress Cataloging in Publications Data

Pieroway, P. Ann
A Taste of Cranberries

1. Cookery (Cranberries)

ISBN: 978-0-9755794-1-X
First printing 2007
Second printing 2008
Third printing 2010

Manufactured in U.S.A.

Phoebe's Kitchen™

Other Books By P. Ann Pieroway
Taste and Tales of Massachusetts
Taste and Tales of Cape Cod
Taste and Tales of Coastal New England
A Taste of Lobsters and some tales too...

Dedication

This book is dedicated to
my late adopted Aunts
Barbara "Mac" Kennedy,
Josephine "Polly" Capillo, and
chef extraordinaire Mafalda "Muffy" Polloni
of Gloucester and Rockport, MA.

A portion of the profits from books by Bass Pond Press will be dedicated to selected projects that will benefit the libraries, gardens and parks of Massachusetts.

Whatever the regional differences, one thing is constant all over the nation—the cranberry. The red berry is jellied and cut in quivering slices, stewed and served with whole berries, squeezed and poured into glasses as a cocktail; nationwide it is spiked with spirits, baked in bread, chopped into a relish, embalmed in gelatin or cubed in a salad.

Horace Sutton,
Saturday Review, November 26, 1977

Table of Contents

*"The cranberry gets its name from
Dutch and German settlers, who
nicknamed it the "crane berry"
after the shape of the blossoms.
When the vines bloom in the late
spring and the flowers' light pink
petals twist back they have a
resemblance to the head
and bill of a crane.
Over time, the name was
shortened to cranberry."*

The Ubiquitous Cranberry

Fresh cranberries are available in late September through December.

SELECTION TIPS
- While most cranberries are purchased in 12 oz. bags, look for berries that are a deep intense red.
- Discard any berries that are soft, shriveled or discolored. Remove any stems.
- Do not wash berries until you are ready to use them as the increase moisture will cause berries to spoil faster.

STORAGE TIPS
- Fresh cranberries can be stored in the refrigerator 4-8 weeks.
- Cranberries freeze very well. I half the berries and freeze them in 1 cup zip-loc packages. This way if I want to bake muffins or bread, I simply use one of the packages.
- Feel free to substitute frozen for fresh berries.

COOKING TIPS
- If cooking, remove from heat when berries begin to "pop". A berry "pops" when its outer skin has expanded and bursts or "pops".

HEALTH BENEFITS
- Excellent source of vitamin A and C, potassium and other minerals; low in sodium.
- Low in calories at only 46 per cup.
- High in antioxidants
- High in fiber. Helps lower cholesterol and aids in digestion.
- Helps prevent urinary tract infections.

It has been an unchallenged doctrine that cranberry sauce, a pink goo of overtones of sugared tomatoes, is a delectable necessity of the Thanksgiving board and that turkey is uneatable without it... There are some things in every country that you must be born to endure; and another hundred years of general satisfaction with Americans and America could not reconcile this expatriate to cranberry sauce, peanut butter, and drum majorettes.

Alistair Cooke, Talk about America

STARTERS

Appetizers

Beverages

Soups

Salads

*While beautiful pictures
show cranberries floating on water,
they do not grow in water.
The cranberry vine is a perennial
plant that grows in bogs
(Massachusetts) and marshes
(Wisconsin). In the fall, some bogs
are flooded for harvesting.
Others are harvested using
machines that resemble
lawnmowers that "comb" the
cranberries.
In Massachusetts the native
cranberry is grown while in
Wisconsin, more hybrids are
grown, which partially explains
the larger harvests.*

Merry, Merry Meatballs

2 pounds extra-lean ground beef
⅓ cup fresh parsley, chopped
2 eggs
⅓ cup ketchup
1 cup dry breadcrumbs
2 tablespoons soy sauce
½ teaspoon garlic salt
¼ teaspoon black pepper
2 tablespoons grated onion
1 (16-ounce) can jellied cranberry sauce
1 (12-ounce) bottle chili sauce
2 tablespoons brown sugar, firmly packed
1 tablespoon lemon juice

1. Preheat oven to 350 degrees F.
2. Combine first nine ingredients in a large bowl.
   With hands, mix well. Form into 1-inch balls.
3. Place meatballs on rack of broiler pan.
4. Bake 10 to 15 minutes until brown.
5. For sauce, combine cranberry sauce, chili sauce,
   brown sugar and lemon juice in a large saucepan
   for 5 minutes.
6. Add cooked meatballs to saucepan and continue
   heating over medium heat for 15 minutes.
7. When ready to serve, transfer to chafing dish.
   Serve with toothpicks.

Yields: 48 to 60 meatballs

Christmas Memories Cookbook

Spicy Cranberry Drumsticks

½ cup jellied cranberry sauce
2 tablespoons hot pepper sauce
1 tablespoon chili sauce
½ teaspoon sea salt
20 chicken drumsticks or chicken wings

1. Preheat oven to 400 degrees F.
2. Combine first four ingredients in a large resealable plastic bag; mix well. Add chicken. Seal and turn bag to coat chicken. Refrigerate at least 1 hour or overnight.
3. Pour chicken and marinade in ungreased 13 x 9-inch baking dish. Bake 40 minutes turning 2 or 3 times and brush with marinade.
4. Transfer chicken pieces to serving dish; discard any remaining marinade.

Serves 8-10

Tangy Cranberry Dip

1 can whole berry cranberry sauce
⅔ cup chili sauce
2 tablespoons horseradish
2 tablespoons dry red wine

1. In a bowl, mix together cranberry sauce, chili sauce, horseradish, and dry red wine; chill.
2. Serve as a dip with ham, chicken or shrimp.

Yields: 2 cups

Brie and Cranberry Appetizers

1 pound prepared phyllo dough
¾ to 1 cup butter, melted
1 (16-ounce) can whole cranberry sauce
2 pound brie cheese, cut into cubes

1. Preheat oven to 350 degrees F.
2. Cut phyllo dough in half lengthwise. Keep covered with plastic wrap while working.
3. Place 2 sheets of phyllo dough on a work surface; brush with melted butter. Fold in half lengthwise; brush with butter.
4. Place 1½ teaspoons cranberry sauce and 6 cubes of brie at the bottom of the strip of dough. Fold the corner over the filling. Fold up, then over the opposite way, forming a triangle. Continue folding in this way until reaching the end of the strip of dough. Brush with butter and place on a jelly roll pan. Repeat with remaining phyllo dough and fillings.
5. Bake for 10 minutes or until golden brown. Cool for 5 minutes before serving.

Yields: 20 to 25 appetizers

Cranberry Glazed Brie

3 cups cranberries
¾ cup brown sugar, firmly packed
⅓ cup dried currants
⅓ water
⅛ dry mustard
⅛ ground allspice
⅛ ground cardamom
⅛ ground cloves
⅛ ground ginger
1 (5-pound) Brie cheese wheel
1 large round loaf of rye or sourdough
4 cups sliced almonds

1. Combine cranberries, brown sugar, currants, water, mustard and spices in heavy non-reactive saucepan.
2. Cook over medium-high heat until most of berries pop, stirring frequently, about 5 minutes. Cool to room temperature.
3. Preheat oven to 325 degrees F.
4. Slice off ½" from top of 7" round bread using a serrated knife. Reserve top of bread.
5. Place Brie on top of bread; trace around outer edge of cheese with knife. Using traced mark as a guide, carefully cut bread vertically 2" deep (do not cut through bread); remove bread.
6. Remove white rind from top of Brie with serrated knife. Place Brie cheese in cavity.
7. Spread top with cranberry mixture and sprinkle with sliced almonds.
8. Bake for 15 to 20 minutes or just until soft.
9. Serve immediately with fresh fruit slices, crackers, chips, or cubed bread.

Serves 12

Taste and Tales of Massachusetts

"If all the cranberry bogs in North America were put together, they would comprise an area equal in size to the tiny island of Nantucket, off the coast of Massachusetts, which is approximately 47 square miles.
If you strung all the cranberries produced in North America last year, they would stretch from Boston to Los Angeles more than 565 times."

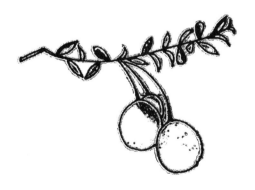

Mulled Cranberry Tea

5 tea bags
2½ cups boiling water
3 cups cranberry juice cocktail
1½ cups water
2 tablespoons honey
½ cup light brown sugar
1 (4-inch) cinnamon stick
8 whole cloves
Sliced lemon or orange

1. Brew tea in boiling water for 10 minutes. Put spices, sugar & honey into a crock pot or large pan. Add cranberry juice cocktail & water.
2. Simmer for at least ten minutes to activate spices.
3. Add tea & sliced fruit. Serve hot or cold.

Yields: 14 - 4 ounce servings

Cook's Note: Mulling spices may be substituted for cinnamon sticks, cloves and fruit slices. Wine or liquor may be added for a hot toddy.

*The first printed recipe for
cranberry juice appeared in 1683
in a cookbook that was called the
"Compleat Cooks Guide"*

Cranberry Mojito

1 cup fresh mint, trimmed
½ cup sugar
1¾ cups light rum
1¼ cups fresh lime juice
¾ cup frozen cranberry juice
   concentrate, thawed
2 (10-ounce) bottles chilled sparkling water
6 cups ice

1. Using a mortar or wooden spoon, mash fresh mint with sugar in a large pitcher.
2. Add rum and fresh lime juice, stirring to dissolve sugar.
3. Mix in cranberry juice concentrate and sparkling water; mix in ice.

Yields: 6 servings

The first cranberries were exported from Massachusetts in the 1820's to Europe. In 2006 over $78 million dollars worth of cranberries were exported from the United States.

Cranberry Orange Punch

2 cups orange juice, chilled
2 quarts cranberry juice, chilled
2 cans frozen strawberry-lemon juice
3 cups pineapple juice
1 quart chilled ginger ale
1 pint sherbet

1. Combine first four ingredients in a 4-quart punch bowl, stir and chill.
2. Fill two old-fashion glasses with ice and pour ½ cup of mixture into each glass.
3. Garnish with slices of lemon, lime and orange.

Yields: 20 5-ounce servings

Cook's Note: Fill ring-shape mold with water and a few slices of lime and lemon; freeze.

Cape Codder

1 cup cranberry juice cocktail
2 cup vodka
4 tablespoons Grand Marnier
4 teaspoons lime juice

1. Mix all ingredients in pitcher, stir to blend.
2. Fill two glasses with ice and pour ½ of mixture into each glass.
3. Garnish with lime wedge.

Serves 2

Hot Cranberry Tea

1 (32-ounce) bottle of cranberry juice cocktail
1 package red hots
1 small can lemonade concentrate
1 small can orange juice concentrate
2 cups sugar
3 quarts water

1. Boil 2 quarts water, sugar, and red hots until sugar and red hots are dissolved.
2. Add cranberry juice cocktail, orange and lemonade concentrate; add 1 quart water. Serve hot.

Yields: 1 gallon

Cranberry Sparkler

2 cups cranberry juice drink, chilled
2 cups raspberry liqueur
1 (750-milliliter) bottle champagne
chilled red raspberries

1. Combine juice drink and liqueur in a large pitcher; add champagne.
2. Serve over ice. Garnish with raspberries.

Yields: 8 cups

Spiced Cranberry Cider

1 quart apple cider
3 cups cranberry juice drink
2 tablespoons brown sugar
2 (3-inch) cinnamon sticks
¾ teaspoon whole cloves
¼ teaspoon ground nutmeg
½ lemon, thinly sliced

1. In a large saucepan, heat all ingredients to a boil over high heat. Reduce heat and simmer 5 to 20 minutes.
2. Remove spices and lemon.
3. Ladle hot cider into mugs or cool to room temperature and serve over ice. Garnish with a cinnamon, if desired.

Yields: 7 cups

Cook's Note: If using cranberry juice cocktail, reduce amount of brown sugar.

Since the Indians referred to the berries as sassamanesh, no one was sure when the name cranberries came into being, but a researcher found a sermon by Massachusetts minister John Eliot, "Apostle to the Indians," said, "Why are Strawberries sweet and Cranberries sowre?"

Mr. Funk of New Orleans

Created by the famous Brennan's Restaurant in honor of their late cellar master Herman Funk.

1 (750-milliliter) bottle champagne, chilled
2½ cups cranberry juice drink, chilled
⅓ to ½ cup peach schnapps
garnish: fresh strawberries

1. Combine champagne, cranberry juice, and schnapps. Pour into stemmed glass.
2. Garnish with fresh strawberries

Serves 4–6

Cranberry Nectar Smoothies

10 ounces strawberries, chilled
1 small banana
1½ cups cranberry nectar, chilled

1. Trim and halve strawberries. Slice banana.
2. In a blender puree strawberries, banana, and cranberry nectar until smooth. Serve immediately, over ice.

Serves 2

Cranberry-Raspberry Soup

8 ounces cranberries, fresh or frozen
1 cup water
½ cup sugar, or more as needed
3 cups raspberries, fresh or frozen
   grated zest and juice of 1 orange
1 cup half-and-half

1. In a large saucepan, combine cranberries, water, and sugar. Bring to a boil, reduce heat, and simmer for 5 minutes. (Many berries will pop.) Remove from heat and cool to room temperature.
2. Stir in raspberries, orange zest, and juice. Pass mixture through a food mill or fine sieve set over a large bowl to remove seeds and cranberry skins. Discard seeds and skins.
3. Whisk half-and-half into soup and taste for sweetness. Add more sugar, if desired. Serve chilled.

Serves 6

Veggie Life Magazine

*"The cranberry is one of three fruits that are native to North America.
The others are blueberries and Concord grapes."*

Cranberry Soup

2 tablespoons butter
½ cup onions, roughly chopped
½ cup celery, chopped
¼ cup carrots, chopped
2½ cups chicken broth
1 small dried hot red pepper
1 bay leaf
1 (12 ounce) bag cranberries
3 cups apple cider
2 tablespoons orange juice
   Freshly ground black pepper, to taste
sour cream to garnish

1. In a heavy soup pan, melt butter.
2. Sauté onions, celery and carrots until soft; add chicken broth.
3. Add hot pepper to broth, together with bay leaf and several grinds of pepper.
4. Rinse and pick cranberries. Roughly chop berries and add to broth. Simmer gently over low heat until berries are soft and disintegrating into broth.
5. Add apple cider and orange juice to broth. Mix well and simmer gently for 10 minutes.
6. Serve hot, garnish with sour cream, if desired.

Serves 6-8

Belgian Endive and Apple Salad
with Cranberry Vinaigrette

2 tablespoons extra virgin olive oil
2 tablespoons frozen cranberry juice
  concentrate, thawed
1 tablespoon white wine vinegar
3 heads Belgian endive, thinly sliced crosswise
2 Red Delicious or Fuji apples,
  unpeeled, cored, chopped
½ cup chopped fresh cranberries
¼ cup thinly sliced green onions
¼ cup walnuts, toasted, coarsely chopped

1 Whisk oil, cranberry juice concentrate and vinegar
   in small bowl to blend. Season to taste with salt
   and pepper.
2. Combine endive and apples in medium bowl. Pour
   dressing over; toss to coat.
3. Sprinkle cranberries, green onions and walnuts
   over and serve.

Serves 4

*In the U.S.A., cranberries are grown
in Wisconsin, Massachusetts,
New Jersey, Oregon and Washington
State. In Canada, farmers
grow cranberries in British
Columbia, New Brunswick,
Ontario, Nova Scotia, and Quebec.
Chile, Estonia, Latvia, Lithuania,
and eastern Europe
also produce cranberries.*

Cranberry Vinaigrette

¼ cup cranberries
½ cup cranberry juice cocktail
1 tablespoon honey
1 teaspoon red wine vinegar
1 tablespoon extra-virgin olive oil
sea salt and pepper

1. In a small saucepan, simmer the fresh cranberries in the cranberry juice reducing by half, about 5 minutes.
2. Transfer to a blender and let cool.
3. Add the honey and red wine vinegar; season with salt and pepper and puree. With the machine on, blend in the olive oil.

Yields: 1 cup

Baby Spinach Salad

1 pound of baby spinach
¾ cup sweetened dried cranberries
1 tablespoon of poppy seeds
¼ cup of white sugar (or sugar substitute)
¼ cup red wine vinegar
¼ cup olive oil

1. Combine the spinach & sweetened dried cranberries in a salad bowl.
2. Combine the poppy seeds & dressing ingredients.
3. Toss with spinach & sweetened dried cranberries, when ready to serve.

Serves 6-8

Cranberry, Bacon and Avocado Salad

3 handfuls baby spinach
6 pieces bacon, cooked until crispy
¼ cup pinenuts, toasted
½ cup sweetened dried cranberries
2 green onions, sliced
1 avocado, roughly diced
2 teaspoons red wine vinegar
⅓ cup olive oil

1. Place salad leaves in a wide, shallow bowl or on a platter.
2. Add bacon to salad. Toss pinenuts, dried cranberries, green onions, and avocado with spinach.
3. Mix red wine vinegar with olive oil; drizzle over salad and serve.

Serves 4

*"The Native Americans referred to the berries as sassamanesh and ibimi. The English called them marsh-whorts, fen-whorts, fen-berries, marsh-berries, or moss-berries.
The Delaware Indians considered the cranberry to be a symbol of peace."*

Cranberry Cashew Salad

1 large head romaine lettuce
1 cup shredded Parmesan cheese
1 cup cashews
¼ cup sweetened dried cranberries
1 red apple, cubed
1 Anjou pear, cubed
½ cup sugar or Splenda™
½ teaspoon sea salt
½ cup lemon juice
⅔ cup olive oil
1 tablespoon poppy seeds
1 teaspoon Dijon mustard

1. In a large bowl, combine lettuce, cheese, cashews, dried cranberries, apple and pear.
2. In a covered container, combine sugar, salt, lemon juice, olive oil, poppy seeds, and Dijon mustard.
3. Shake vigorously until well mixed. Wait until ready to serve to add dressing to salad. Pour over salad and toss to coat evenly.

Serves 4

Summer Fruit Salad

1 can mandarin oranges, drained
1 can pineapple chunks, drained,
   reserve ½ cup juice
1 large banana, sliced
2 kiwi fruit, sliced
1 cup sweetened dried cranberries
1 tablespoon fresh lime juice
1 tablespoon fresh lemon juice
2 tablespoons honey

1. Slice banana into the combined lime and lemon
   juice; stir to coat bananas; add honey.
2. Add honey. Add reserved pineapple and rest of
   fruit. Stir gently just to mix fruit & juices.
3. Serve on salad greens or as a dessert with
   whipped cream.

Serves 6

*Mention of the use of cranberries
began right at the beginning.
John Josselyn, said that "The
Indians and English use them
much, boyling them with sugar for
sauce to eat with their Meat, and it
is a delicate Sauce."
Other accounts mention
the Indians using cranberries with
maple syrup or honey.*

Cranberry-Apple Turkey Salad

¼ cup low-fat vanilla yogurt
2 tablespoons light mayonnaise
2½ cups boneless, skinless turkey breast, diced
½ cup dried cranberries
1 medium celery rib, chopped
¼ cup red onion, finely chopped
2 tablespoons pecans, chopped
2 medium apples, sliced

1. In a medium bowl, stir together yogurt and mayonnaise.
2. Stir in turkey and remaining ingredients, except apples.
3. Place lettuce on individual salad plates; using ice cream scoop put one scoop of turkey on top of lettuce.
4. Garnish with sliced apples.

Serves 4

*We have from the time called May
until Michaelmas* a great store of
very good wild fruits as
strawberries, cranberries and
hurtleberries. The cranberries,
much like cherries for color and
bigness, may be kept until fruit
comes in again. An excellent sauce
is made of them for venison,
turkeys and other great fowl and
they are better to make tarts than
either gooseberries or cherries. We
have them brot to our homes by
the Indians in great plenty.*

Mahon Stacy, April 26, 1680 (New Jersey)
in a letter to his brother in England.

*A festival celebrated on September 29 in honor of the Archangel Michael.

BREADS

Biscuits

Fritters

Scones

Biscotti

Muffins

*Did you know that cranberries
have two crops—
the less know summer crop and the
well known fall harvest?
During the summer the fruit of
many varieties are very light
or white in color.
In the past, this crop
known as "snowfalls"
was discarded so that the fall
harvest could flourish.
Today, due to its mild light flavor
it is used for white cranberry juice.*

Cranberry Bread

2 tablespoons butter
1 cup sugar
1 tablespoon orange peel, grated
¾ cup orange juice
1 egg, beaten
2 cups all-purpose flour
1½ teaspoons baking powder
1 teaspoon sea salt
½ teaspoon baking soda
1 cup fresh cranberries, quartered

1. Preheat oven to 350 degrees F. Grease and flour 1 large loaf pan or 12 cup muffin tin.
2. Cream butter and sugar in large bowl. Add grated orange peel, juice, and egg. Mix well.
3. In separate bowl sift flour, baking powder, salt and baking soda. Gradually add to large bowl, beating until smooth. Do not over mix. Stir in the cranberries.
4. Pour in either loaf pan or muffin tin.
5. Bake bread for 55 minutes and the muffins for 30 minutes. Check with tester to make sure bread is done.

Yields: 1 large loaf or 12 muffins

Taste and Tales of Massachusetts

Cranberry Biscuits

2 cups unbleached all-purpose flour
2½ teaspoons baking powder
2 teaspoons sugar
1 teaspoon sea salt
5 tablespoons cold unsalted butter,
   cut into small pieces
½ cup dried cranberries, snipped
1 cup buttermilk
1 egg, lightly beaten

1. Preheat oven to 400 degrees F.
2. Line a baking sheet with parchment paper.
3. In a large bowl, combine flour, baking powder, sugar and salt; cut-in pieces of butter until it is the size of small peas.
4. Add dried cranberries, buttermilk and egg; mix well. Dough will be sticky.
5. Transfer to a floured surface and knead dough until it is smooth. Do not over-knead. Pat into a round shape about ½ - inch thick.
6. Using a 2-inch round biscuit cutter, cut out biscuits and place on parchment paper. Gather pieces and repeat until all pieces are used. Brush top with beaten egg. Bake for 15 minutes or until tops are golden. Serve immediately.

Yields: about 2 dozen biscuits

Cranberry Fritters

1 cup cranberries
¼ cup sugar
½ cup water
2 cups all-purpose flour
¾ cup sugar
1 teaspoon baking powder
2 eggs, separated
¼ cup ice water
1 apple, peeled and diced
confectioners sugar
raspberry jam
oil for frying

1. In a saucepan, combine cranberries, sugar and water. Over high heat, cook until berries begin to burst. Remove from heat and chill.
2. Sift together flour, sugar and baking powder. Beat egg yolks with ice water. Add the sifted dry ingredients, apple, cranberries and any liquid in the pan used to cook them.
3. In a separate bowl, beat egg whites until soft peaks form. Fold into cranberry mixture.
4. In a deep skillet or deep fat fryer, heat 1 or 2 inches of oil to 350 degrees. For each fritter, drop 2 tablespoons of batter into the oil. Cook 1 minute, flip the fritters over, and continue frying until golden. This may have to be done in batches; be sure oil returns to 350 degrees between batches.
5. Drain fritters on paper towels and dust with confectioners sugar. Serve with raspberry jam.

Serves 6

Cranberry Scones

2 cups all-purpose flour
½ cup sugar
½ teaspoon baking powder
¼ teaspoon baking soda
½ teaspoon sea salt
8 tablespoons butter, frozen
½ cup sweetened dry cranberries
½ cup sour cream
1 large egg
1 teaspoon finely grated orange (optional)
½ teaspoon sugar

1. Preheat oven to 400 degrees F.
2. In a medium bowl, mix flour, sugar, baking powder, baking soda and salt.
3. Grate butter into mixture using the large holes of a box grater; use your fingers to work in the butter. The mixture should resemble coarse meal. Then stir in dried cranberries.
4. In a small bowl, whisk sour cream and egg until smooth. Using a fork, stir sour cream mixture into flour mixture until large clumps of dough form. Use your hands to press the dough against the bowl into a ball. (The dough will be sticky at first, and there may not seem to be enough liquid, but as you press, the dough will come together.)
5. Place on a lightly floured surface and pat into a 7- or 8-inch circle about ¾-inch thick. Sprinkle with a teaspoon or two of sugar. Use a sharp knife to cut into 8 triangles.
6. Place on a cookie sheet (preferably lined with parchment paper) about 1 inch apart. Bake about 15 to 17 minutes or until golden. Cool 5 minutes and serve warm or at room temperature.

Yields: 8 scones

Hundreds of years ago, long before the Pilgrims arrived in 1620, the Native Americans mixed deer meat and mashed cranberries to make pemmican. It had a cake like consistency and lasted for long periods of time. Medicine men considered the cranberry to be essential in caring for members of their tribe. It was an important ingredient in poultices that would draw the poison from arrow wounds. Women used the red juice of the cranberry as a natural dye for rugs, blankets and clothing.

Dried Cranberry and
White Chocolate Biscotti

2½ cups all purpose flour
1 teaspoon baking powder
½ teaspoon sea salt
1½ cups sugar
½ cup (1 stick) unsalted butter, room temperature
2 large eggs
½ teaspoon almond extract
1½ cups dried cranberries (about 6 ounces)
1 egg white
6 ounces good-quality white chocolate chopped
   or chips

1. Preheat oven to 350 degrees F. Line heavy large baking sheet with parchment paper.
2. Combine flour, baking powder and salt in medium bowl; whisk to blend.
3. Using electric mixer, beat sugar, butter, eggs and almond extract in large bowl until well blended; add flour mixture, then dried cranberries. Divide dough in half.
4. Using floured hands, shape each piece into 2½-inch wide, 9½-inch-long, 1-inch-high log. Transfer both logs to the baking sheet, spacing evenly.
5. Whisk egg white in small bowl until foamy; brush egg white glaze on top and sides of each log. Bake logs until golden brown (logs will spread), about 35 minutes. Cool completely on sheet on rack. Maintain oven temperature.
6. Transfer logs to work surface. Discard parchment. Using serrated knife, cut logs on diagonal into ½ inch-wide slices. Arrange slices, cut side down, on same sheet.

7. Bake 10 minutes; turn biscotti over. Bake until just beginning to color, about 5 minutes. Transfer biscotti to rack.
8. Stir chocolate in top of double boiler over simmering water until smooth. Remove from over water. Using fork, drizzle chocolate over biscotti. Let stand until chocolate sets, about 30 minutes.

Makes about 28.

Adapted from Bon Appetit!

The milk drops on your chin,
Helga, Must not interfere with the
cranberry red of your cheek Nor
the sky winter blue of your eyes.

Carl Sandburg (1878 – 1967),
Smoke and Steel, 1922

Cranberry Sour Cream Coffee Cake

1 cup (2 sticks) butter
1 cup sugar
2 eggs
1 teaspoon baking powder
1 teaspoon baking soda
½ cup chopped walnuts or pecans
1 (8-ounce) can whole cranberry sauce
2 cups all-purpose flour, sifted
½ teaspoon sea salt
½ pint sour cream
1 teaspoon almond flavoring

1. Preheat oven to 350 degrees F. Grease and flour a bundt pan.
2. Cream butter; add sugar and unbeaten eggs, one at a time.
3. Add dry ingredients alternating with sour cream ending with dry ingredients; add almond flavoring.
4. Place half of batter in bottom of pan. Add half of can of cranberry sauce and spread evenly.
5. Add remaining batter; spread rest of cranberry sauce on top. Sprinkle with nuts.
6. Bake for 55 minutes or until tester comes out clean.

Glaze:
¾ cups confectioners sugar
2 tablespoons warm water
2 teaspoon almond extract

1. Combine sugar, almond extract, and water.
2. Pour over warm cake and let run.

Cranberries and Cream Muffins

2 cups all-purpose flour
1 cup granulated sugar
1 teaspoon baking powder
½ teaspoon baking soda
½ teaspoon sea salt
1½ cups fresh or frozen cranberries
2 eggs, lightly beaten
1 (8-ounce) carton sour cream
½ cup vegetable oil
½ teaspoon vanilla extract

1. Preheat oven to 400 degrees F. Grease or line muffin cups.
2. In a large bowl combine flour, baking powder, baking soda and salt.
3. Cut cranberries in half and toss gently with dry ingredients.
4. In a small bowl, combine eggs, sour cream, oil and vanilla; mix well. Stir wet ingredients into dry ingredients just until moistened. Fill prepared muffin cups ⅔ full.
5. Bake for 20 to 25 minutes or until muffins test done.

Yields: 12 standard-sized muffins.

Cranberry Pumpkin Muffins

2 cups fresh or frozen cranberries, chopped
2 cups all-purpose flour
¾ cup of granulated sugar
3 teaspoons baking powder
1 teaspoon sea salt
½ teaspoon ground cinnamon
½ teaspoon ground allspice
⅓ cup cooking oil
2 eggs
¾ cup canned pumpkin

1. Preheat oven to 400 degrees F.
2. Sift all dry ingredients together; set aside.
3. Beat oil, eggs and pumpkin until well blended and add all at once to dry ingredients.
4. Stir just until moistened; fold in cranberries.
5. Spoon into paper lined muffin cups.
6. Bake for 25-30 min.

Yields: 18 muffins.

Well, art is art, isn't it. Still, on the other hand, Water is water! And east is east, and west is west and if you take cranberries and stew them like applesauce they taste much more like prunes than rhubarb does.

Groucho Marx

Cranberry Streusel Muffins

2 cups all-purpose flour
1 cup packed brown sugar
½ cup (1 stick) butter
3 tablespoons walnuts, finely chopped
2 teaspoons baking powder
½ teaspoon baking soda
½ teaspoon sea salt
1 teaspoon nutmeg
½ teaspoon orange rind, grated
2 eggs, beaten
¾ cup buttermilk
1 cup fresh cranberries, chopped
½ cup chopped walnuts

1. Preheat oven to 375 degrees F. Grease 18 muffin tins.
2. Mix 1 cup flour and brown sugar in bowl. Cut in butter until crumbly. Reserve ½ cup mixture.
3. Mix finely chopped walnuts into reserved crumb mixture; set aside.
4. Add remaining cup flour, baking powder, baking soda, salt, nutmeg and orange rind to remaining crumb mixture. Beat eggs with buttermilk.
5. Add to flour mixture; mix just until moistened. Stir in cranberries and walnuts.
6. Fill tins ¾ full; sprinkle top with reserved crumb mixture.
7. Bake 20 to 25 minutes.

Yields: 18 muffins

*In the 1870s, growers in Wisconsin
lost a great many cranberries due
to flooding and freezing weather.
As growers installed irrigation
systems, they learned that loses due
to frost could be minimized by
flooding the marshes.
Today, owners now sprinkle the
water over the cranberry plants to
prevent frost damage
(in Florida they do the same
for the strawberry and
orange crops.)*

YUMMIES

Candy
Cookies
Puddings
Cakes
Desserts
Pies

Valentines Fudge

2 cups semi-sweet chocolate chips
¼ cup light corn syrup
½ cup confectioners sugar
¼ cup evaporated milk
1 teaspoon vanilla or almond extract flavoring
¾ cup of sweetened dried cranberries
½ cup chopped walnuts or toasted almonds

1. Line the bottom of an 8 X 8 inch pan with plastic wrap. Set aside.
2. Melt chocolate chips and corn syrup over very low heat or in a double boiler, stirring frequently. When very smooth remove from heat.
3. Stir in confectioners sugar, evaporated milk and flavoring. Beat until the mixture is thick and shiny.
4. Add nuts and sweetened dried cranberries and mix well.
5. Pour into prepared pan. Cool to room temperature, cover and refrigerate several hours or until firm. Cut into squares. Store covered in the refrigerator.

Yields: 25 small squares.

"There are four unbroken rules
when it comes to Thanksgiving:
there must be turkey and dressing,
cranberries, mashed potatoes,
and pumpkin pie."

John Hadamuscin, 'Down Home' (1993)

Chocolate Covered Cranberries

12 ounces of whole cranberries
12 ounces milk chocolate chips
2 tablespoons shortening

1. Melt chocolate chips and shortening over low heat, stirring frequently until melted.
2. Dip cranberries in chocolate with toothpick until coated.
3. Place on wax paper. Refrigerate until firm.

Wisconsin Cranberry Growers Association

Cranberry Nut Bar

2 eggs
1 cup sugar
1 cup all-purpose flour
⅓ cup butter, melted
1¼ cups fresh cranberries
½ cup nuts, chopped

1. Preheat oven to 350 degrees F.
2. Beat eggs well, add sugar gradually, beating until well blended.
3. Stir in flour and melted butter; blend well.
4. Add cranberries and walnuts and mix gently.
5. Spread in greased 8-inch pan.
6. Bake for 45 minutes or until golden.

Yields: 16 squares

Favorite Recipes of Northampton

Cranberry Orange Oatmeal Cookies

1 cup (2 sticks) butter, softened
1 cup brown sugar, firmly packed
½ cup granulated sugar
2 eggs
1 teaspoon vanilla
1½ cups all-purpose flour
1 teaspoon baking soda
1 teaspoon cinnamon
½ teaspoon sea salt
2 tablespoons orange juice
3 cups oats, uncooked
1 cup dried cranberries

1. Heat oven to 350 degrees F.
2. Beat together butter and sugars until creamy.
3. Add eggs and vanilla; beat well.
4. Add combined flour, baking soda, cinnamon and salt; mix well. Add orange juice and mix well.
5. Stir in oats and cranberries; mix well.
6. Drop by rounded tablespoons onto ungreased cookie sheet.
7. Bake 8 to 10 minutes for chewy cookies; 10 to 12 minutes for more cake like cookies.

Yields: 48 cookies

Oatmeal Cranberry
White Chocolate Chunk Cookies

⅔ cup butter, softened
⅔ cup brown sugar
2 eggs
1½ cups old fashioned oats
1½ cups all-purpose flour
1 teaspoon baking soda
½ teaspoon sea salt
1 (6 ounce) package sweetened dried cranberries
⅔ cup white chocolate chunks or chips

1. Preheat oven to 375 degrees F.
2. Using an electric mixer, beat butter and sugar together in a medium mixing bowl until light and fluffy.
3. Add eggs; mix well.
4. Combine oats, flour, baking soda and salt in a separate mixing bowl.
5. Add to butter mixture in several additions, mixing well after each addition.
6. Stir in dried cranberries and white chocolate chunks.
7. Bake 8 to 10 minutes for chewy cookies; 10 to12 minutes for more cake like cookies.

Yields: 4 dozen cookies

Cranberry-Pecan Rugalach

1 cup (2 sticks) butter, softened
1 (8-ounce) package cream cheese, softened
½ cup granulated sugar
2¾ cups all-purpose flour
½ teaspoon sea salt
¾ cup sugar
⅔ cup toasted pecans, chopped
⅔ cup dried cranberries, finely chopped
½ cup butter, melted
1½ teaspoons ground cinnamon
¾ teaspoon ground allspice
1 large egg, lightly beaten
½ cup sparkling sugar

1. Beat butter and cream cheese at medium speed with an electric mixer until creamy; gradually add granulated sugar, beating until fluffy. Stir in flour and salt.
2. Divide dough into 8 equal portions; flatten each portion into a disk; wrap each disk separately in plastic wrap. Chill 8 hours.
3. To make the Cranberry-Pecan Filling, stir together sugar, toasted pecans, dried cranberries, melted butter, cinnamon and allspice until blended.
4. Roll 1 portion of dough at a time into an 8-inch circle on a lightly floured surface.
5. Spread 3 tablespoons of filling on disk, leaving a ½-inch border. Cut circle into 8 wedges; roll up wedges, starting at wide end, to form a crescent shape

6. Place point side down, on a lightly greased baking sheet. Brush gently with egg; sprinkle with sparkling sugar. Repeat steps 5 and 6.
7. Bake at 350 degrees F for 20 minutes or until golden brown. Remove to wire racks to cool completely.

Yields: 5 dozen

Adapted from Southern Living

Cook's Note: Sparkling sugar can be located along with cake decorating supplies.

In 1930, Ocean Spray was formed as a grower-owned marketing cooperative by three cranberry growers and remains a cooperative today with many hundreds of growers. It is the number one brand of canned and bottled juice drinks in the United States. The first product, cranberry juice, was introduced in 1930 and Cranberry Sauce began gracing America's tables in early 1940.

Cranberry Chews

2 ⅓ cups unbleached all-purpose flour
1 cup brown sugar, packed
1 teaspoon ground cinnamon
½ teaspoon ground nutmeg
¼ teaspoon ground cloves
½ teaspoon sea salt
1 cup (2 sticks) cold butter, sliced
1½ cups quick oats
1 (16-ounce) can whole berry cranberry sauce
½ cup orange marmalade
1 teaspoon vanilla
1 cup chopped walnuts

1. Preheat oven to 350 degrees F.
2. Combine 2 cups flour, brown sugar, spices and salt. Cut in butter with fork or pastry blender until mixture resembles coarse crumbs. Stir in oats. Reserve ½ cup mixture.
3. Firmly press remaining mixture over bottom of greased 10 x 15-inch jellyroll pan.
4. Bake for 15 minutes. Cool 10 minutes before filling.
5. In a medium bowl stir together cranberry sauce, marmalade and vanilla. Add remaining ⅓ cup of flour, 1 tablespoon at a time, blending well after each addition. Spread evenly over cooled crust.
6. Add nuts to reserved 1½ cups crumb mixture. Sprinkle over cranberry filling.
7. Bake another 30 minutes or until lightly browned. Cool in pan on rack.

Yields: about 5 dozen

Cranberry Pudding

2 cups fresh cranberries
¾ cup sugar
¼ cup walnuts, coarsely chopped
6 tablespoons butter, melted
1 egg, well beaten
½ cup flour
vanilla ice cream

1. Preheat oven to 350 degrees F.
2. Place cranberries in a well-buttered 8-inch pie plate.
3. Mix ¼ cup sugar with the nuts and 4 tablespoons of the melted butter and pour over the cranberries.
4. To the beaten egg add the remaining ½ cup sugar combined with the flour, then add the remaining 2 tablespoons melted butter.
5. Beat a bit more. Pour over berry mixture.
6. Bake 45 minutes.
7. Serve warm with a scoop of vanilla ice cream on top of each serving.

Serves 6

The Martha's Vineyard Cookbook

Massachusetts named the cranberry the State berry in 1994 and ten years later in 2004, Wisconsin's Governor signed legislation designating the cranberry the State berry.

Cranberry Pineapple Bars

1 cup cranberries
3 tablespoons brown sugar
1½ teaspoons cornstarch
1 (8-ounce) can crushed pineapple in juice,
  undrained
¾ cup all-purpose flour
¾ cup quick-cooking oats, uncooked
¼ cup brown sugar, firmly packed
¼ teaspoon ground ginger
¼ teaspoon ground cinnamon
3 tablespoons butter, cut into small pieces
  and chilled
1 egg white, lightly beaten
vegetable cooking spray
3 tablespoons pecans, chopped

1. Combine first 4 ingredients in a medium saucepan;
   stir well. Bring to a boil over medium heat; cook
   1minute. Cover, reduce heat, and simmer 12
   minutes or until cranberry skins pop and mixture
   thickens, stirring occasionally. Set aside.
2. Preheat oven to 350 degrees F.
3. Combine flour and next 4 ingredients in a bowl,
   cut in chilled butter with a pastry blender until
   mixture resembles coarse meal.
4. Reserve ½ cup oat mixture. Combine remaining oat
   mixture and egg white; stir well. Press oat mixture
   into bottoms of an 8 inch square baking pan
   coated with cooking spray.
5. Bake for 10 minutes

6. Spread cranberry mixture over prepared crust. Combine reserved oat mixture and pecans; sprinkle over cranberry mixture. Return to oven and bake for 30 minutes or until golden brown.
7. Cool completely in pan on a wire rack.

Yields: 16 bars (2-inch squares)

Burgundy Pie

1 cup sugar
3 tablespoons cornstarch
dash sea salt
1½ cups cranberries
2 cups blueberries fresh or frozen
pastry for 2 crust pie

1. Preheat oven to 425 degrees F.
2. Combine sugar, cornstarch and salt.
3. Stir into mixed berries.
4. Spread into pastry-lined pie pan. Place top crust on, adjust and flute.
5. Bake for 1 hour.

Serves 8-10

Cranberry Spoonbread

2 cups dried cranberries
1 cup yellow cornmeal
½ cup sugar
1 teaspoon grated orange rind
¼ teaspoon sea salt
¼ teaspoon ground cinnamon
3 cups milk
¼ cup (½ stick) butter, melted
4 large eggs, separated
1½ teaspoon baking powder
1 tablespoon powdered sugar

1. Preheat oven to 350 degrees F.
2. Combine first 6 ingredients in a saucepan; stir in milk and butter. Cook over medium heat, stirring constantly, until thickened and bubbly. Remove from heat; cool 5 minutes. Stir in egg yolks and baking powder.
3. Beat egg whites at high speed with an electric mixer until stiff peaks form; fold one-third into cornmeal mixture. Fold in remaining egg whites.
4. Spoon mixture into a lightly greased 2½-quart baking dish; place dish on a baking sheet.
5. Bake for 50 minutes or until puffed and golden, shielding with aluminum foil after 20 minutes to prevent excessive browning.
6. Sprinkle with powdered sugar, and serve immediately.

Serves: 10-12

Cranberry Streusel

4 cups apples peeled and chopped
2 cups fresh cranberries
1½ teaspoons lemon juice
1 cup sugar
⅓ cup brown sugar, firmly packed
1 cup chopped walnuts
1⅓ cup oats, uncooked
½ cup (1 stick) butter, melted
vanilla ice cream

1. Preheat oven to 350 degrees F.
2. Combine apple and cranberries in a lightly buttered 2-quart baking dish. Sprinkle with lemon juice, top with sugar.
3. Combine oats, walnuts, brown sugar, and butter. Stir mixture until dry ingredients are just moistened and mixture is crumbly. Sprinkle over fruit.
4. Bake for one hour.
5. Serve warm with vanilla ice cream.

Serves: 8

*A barrel of cranberries weighs
100 pounds. There are about
450 cranberries in a pound,
4,400 in one gallon of freshly
pressed juice and
45,000 cranberries
in a 100-pound barrel.*

Lemon Cranberry Pound Cake

1 cup (2 sticks) butter, softened
1½ cups sugar
4 eggs
1 teaspoon vanilla
2 tablespoons grated lemon rind
3 cups flour
2 teaspoons baking powder
½ teaspoon sea salt
1 cup milk
1 cup dried sweetened cranberries
½ cup confectioners sugar, sifted
2 tablespoons lemon juice

1. Preheat oven to 325 degrees F. Grease and flour a 10-inch bundt or tube pan.
2. Beat butter and sugar until light and fluffy. Beat in eggs, one at a time. Add in vanilla and lemon rind.
3. Combine flour, baking powder and salt. Gradually add dry ingredients into mixture alternating with milk just until blended. Stir in cranberries. Spoon batter into pan.
4. Bake for 55 to 60 minutes or until toothpick comes out clean.
5. To make glaze combine the confectioners sugar and lemon juice until sugar dissolves. Pierce cake all over with toothpick; spoon glaze evenly over top of cake. Let cool on rack before removing from pan. Wrap and store at room temperature a day before serving.

Serves 12

Cranberry-Apple Crisp with Oatmeal Streusel Topping

1 cup golden brown sugar, packed
1 cup old-fashioned oats
¾ cup all-purpose flour
¾ teaspoon sea salt
½ cup (1 stick) chilled unsalted butter,
  cut into pieces

Filling:
  2 (12-ounce) packages cranberries
  1¾ pounds Golden Delicious or Fuji apples,
  peeled, cored, cut into ½-inch cubes
  1½ cups sugar
  2 tablespoons apple cider or juice

1. Combine brown sugar, oats, flour and salt in a large bowl; toss to blend.
2. Add butter and rub in with fingertips until mixture comes together in moist clumps. Cover and keep chilled until ready to use.
3. Preheat oven to 155 degrees F. Generously butter 13x9x2-inch glass baking dish.
4. Combine cranberries, apples, sugar and apple juice in heavy large pot. Bring to a boil over medium heat, stirring often.
5. Boil until cranberries are tender and juices thicken slightly, about 5 minutes. Transfer filling to prepared dish. Sprinkle topping over.
6. Bake crisp until filling bubbles and topping is crisp and deep golden brown, about 40 minutes. Let cool 10 minutes. Serve with Ice cream.

Serves 12

Cranberry Ice Cream

1 (12 ounces) package cranberries
¼ cup water
2¾ cups whipping cream
1 cup sugar
few drops vanilla extract

1. Rinse the berries. Put in a non-corroding saucepan with the water and cook, covered, stirring occasionally, for about 10 minutes, or until the berries are soft. Puree through a food mill and strain to remove the seeds. Measure 1¼ cups.
2. Warm the cream with the sugar, stirring occasionally, until the sugar has dissolved. Whisk the puree into the cream mixture and chill. Add a few drops of vanilla to taste and freeze according to the instructions with your ice cream maker.

Yields: 1 quart

In the fall of the year, the cranberry bogs come to life with color. Cranberries do not grow in water; instead they grow on vines in impermeable beds layered with sand, peat, gravel, and clay. Glacial deposits originally made the beds known as "bogs".

Cranberry-Apple-Nut Pie

2 cups fresh cranberries, chopped
2 cups apple chopped and peeled
1–1½ cups sugar
½ cup nuts, chopped
2 tablespoons quick cooking tapioca
¼ teaspoon ground cinnamon
pastry for 9-inch, double-crust pie
milk

1. Preheat oven to 375 degrees F.
2. In a large mixing bowl, combine cranberries, apple, sugar, nuts, tapioca, and cinnamon. Let stand 20 minutes.
3. Turn cranberry mixture into a 9-inch, pastry lined pie plate. Adjust top crust; seal and flute edges. Cuts vents in top crust.
4. Brush top crust with milk and sprinkle with additional sugar, if desired. Cover edge of pie with foil to prevent over browning.
5. Bake or 25 minutes, remove foil. Bake for 20 to 30 minutes more or till golden.

Serves 6-8

Eagle River First Prize Winner

*Since the cranberry is native
to the USA, originally no one
owned the vines, so laws had to be
enacted imposing fines if
cranberries were harvested before
the berries turned red.
A Provincetown, MA ordinance
reads as follow:
"Any person should be found
getting cranberries before ye
twentieth of September exceeding
one quart should be liable to pay
one dollar and have the berrys
taken away."*

ENTREES

Pork

Meat

Poultry

Pork Tenderloin
with Balsamic-Cranberry Sauce

1½ tablespoons butter
1 (8–10 ounces) pork tenderloin
½ cup sweet onion, chopped
1 tablespoon fresh rosemary, chopped
½ cup chicken broth, low-salt
⅓ cup whole berry cranberry sauce
1 tablespoon balsamic vinegar

1. Preheat oven to 450 degrees F.
2. Melt ½ tablespoon butter in heavy ovenproof skillet over medium-high heat. Sprinkle pork tenderloin with salt and pepper. Sear meat on all sides.
3. Place skillet in oven; roast until thermometer inserted in center registers 155 degrees F.
4. Meanwhile, melt remaining butter in heavy skillet over medium-high heat. Add onion and rosemary, sauté until onions are soft. Add broth, cranberry sauce and vinegar and whisk until cranberry sauce melts.
5. Transfer cooked tenderloin to work surface. Scrape any juice from large skillet into cranberry mixture. Boil until sauce has reduced enough to coat spoon. Season with salt and pepper.
6. Slice tenderloin and serve with cranberry sauce.

Serves 2-4

Cook's Note: Delicious with cranberry wild rice and asparagus. Can be doubled.

Cranberry Glazed Ham

1 smoked ham, fully cooked
½ cup whole-berry cranberry sauce
3 tablespoons brown sugar
1 tablespoon spicy brown mustard

1. Preheat oven to 325 degrees F.
2. Place ham on a broiler pan lined with foil. Insert meat thermometer into thickest portion of ham.
3. Score rind of ham in a diamond pattern.
4. Combine cranberry sauce, sugar, and mustard; brush over ham. Bake an additional 35 minutes or until thermometer registers 140 degrees F.
5. Transfer ham to a platter; let stand to 10-15 minutes before slicing.

Serves 8-10

Cook's Note: Sliced thin and serve on small biscuits as an appetizer.

They sail'd to the Western Sea,
they did,
To a land all cover'd with trees:
And they bought an owl,
and a useful cart,
And a pound of rice,
and a cranberry-tart.

Edward Lear, "The Jumblies"

Prosciutto Wrapped
Pork Tenderloin
With Cranberry Marmalade

2 tablespoons vegetable oil
2 large red onions, sliced
½ cup sugar
½ cup fresh cranberries
2 tablespoons Marsala wine
2 tablespoons raspberry vinegar
2 whole pork tenderloins
8 thin slices prosciutto
1 tablespoon vegetable oil

1. Preheat oven to 450 degrees F.
2. For cranberry marmalade, heat 2 tablespoons oil in large skillet over medium-high heat. Add onions; sauté 5 minutes, stirring occasionally.
3. Stir in sugar and cranberries. Continue cooking over medium-high heat, stirring frequently, until onions are very tender and sauce is thickened, about 5 minutes.
4. Add wine and vinegar. Reduce sauce by half, stirring frequently, about 5 minutes.
5. Cut pork tenderloin crosswise into four pieces. Wrap each piece in 2 slices of prosciutto. Squeeze prosciutto-covered pork to help ham adhere to pork. Cut each piece of prosciutto wrapped pork in to 4 pieces.
6. Heat 1 tablespoon oil in large ovenproof skillet over medium-high heat. Brown pork pieces on both sides, about 5 minutes total.

7. Remove skillet from heat and place in oven; roast 6-8 minutes or until nicely browned.
8. To serve, spoon about ⅓ cup warm marmalade onto each of four plates. Top with 4 pork pieces per plate.

Serves 4

Adapted from National Pork Board

In 1816, Captain Henry Hull of Dennis noticed that sand blowing gently over his bog and settling on the cranberry vine improved their product. Other growers soon followed suit and an industry was born. Today, there are more than 14,000 acres of cranberry bogs nestled throughout southeastern Massachusetts.

Cranberry Pot Roast

3 tablespoons all-purpose flour
1 teaspoon sea salt
½ teaspoon black pepper, freshly ground
1 (one) 3 – 4-pound beef pot roast
3 tablespoons oil
1 small yellow onion, sliced thinly lengthwise
1 large clove garlic, minced
4 whole cloves
1 (2-inch) stick cinnamon
½ cup beef broth

1. Combine flour, salt and pepper and rub into pot roast on all sides, using all of the mixture.
2. In Dutch oven, heat oil and slowly brown onions and garlic until translucent and limp in hot oil. Remove from heat. Add cloves, stick cinnamon, pre-cooked onion and garlic and beef broth to pot roast.
3. Cover tightly and simmer about 2-½ hours or until tender, adding more broth, if necessary spoon off fat. Add cranberry sauce and heat through before serving.

Serves 8-10

During World War II,
American troops required about
one million pounds of dehydrated
cranberries a year.

Cranberry Sauce

1 (12-ounce package) cranberries
1 cup water or Pinot Noir wine
1 cup sugar
1 seedless orange with peeling, sliced in circles
   as thinly as possible
6 whole cloves
1 whole cinnamon stick

1. Add sugar to water or wine and bring to a boil.
   Then add cranberries and the rest of the
   ingredients. Allow to come to a boil, then simmer
   gently for 15 to 20 minutes.
2. Cool and add to Pot Roast.

*Former president John Adams
wrote in a diary on April 8, 1767,
"found a fine Wild Goose on the
Spit and Cramberries stewing in
the Skillet for Dinner at Dr. Tuft's.
He added that Tuft invited him "to
dine upon wild goose and
Cramberry Sause."*

Ragout of Beef with Cranberries

1 – 2 tablespoons unsalted butter
1 – 2 tablespoons oil
2 pounds lean stew meat in 1-inch chunks
¾ teaspoon sea salt
pepper to taste
2 large cloves garlic, minced
2 medium onions, chopped
½ pound mushrooms, sliced
¾ cup port or red wine
¾ cup beef broth
2 tablespoons red wine vinegar
1 tablespoon tomato paste
1½ cups cranberries, coarsely chopped
⅓ cup light brown sugar
2 tablespoons all-purpose flour

1. Melt 1 tablespoon butter and oil in Dutch oven.
2. Brown meat well on all sides. Add onions, as needed, then seasonings, garlic and vinegar. Add more oil or butter if necessary.
3. Finally, add mushrooms, wine, broth, vinegar and tomato paste.
4. Bring to boil, reduce heat and simmer covered about 2 hours or until meat is tender.
5. Combine flour and sugar and toss with cranberries. Add to stew and cook another 10 minutes.
6. Serve with noodles.

Serves 6

Christmas Memories Cookbook

Chicken Cranberry

6 chicken breasts
garlic to taste
sea salt and pepper to taste
2 green peppers, sliced
3 onions, sliced
10 mushrooms, sliced
1 can whole berry cranberry sauce
½ cup cider vinegar
1 cup orange juice
1 tablespoon soy sauce
1 tablespoon cornstarch
olive oil
water

1. Sauté chicken breasts in garlic and olive oil until browned on medium-high heat; season with salt and pepper. Remove chicken.
2. Simmer sliced peppers and onions in pan until soft; add mushrooms, cider vinegar, whole cranberry sauce, and orange juice.
3. Return chicken to pan and cook until chicken is tender; remove chicken.
4. Mix cornstarch, soy sauce and water to make a smooth paste; add to sauce and vegetables; stir gently until thickened.
5. Place chicken on bed of cooked white rice; pour vegetables and thickened sauce over all. Garnish with sliced oranges.

Serves 6

Decas Cranberries

Chicken Cape Ann

3 ounces each diced yellow onion and celery
3 ounces fresh or frozen cranberries, diced
1 ounce walnuts, chopped
6 tablespoons butter
2 tablespoons chicken stock
2 tablespoons cranberry juice
1 teaspoon poultry seasoning
8 ounces dry bread with crust, cubed
10 (6-ounce) boneless chicken breasts, flattened
2 cups chicken stock
6 ounces Champagne
1 cup whipping cream
¼ cup butter, cubed
¼ ounce cornstarch
2 tablespoons water
white pepper to taste

1. Sauté the first 4 ingredients in 6 tablespoons butter. Stir in 2 tablespoons chicken stock, cranberry juice, poultry seasoning and white pepper. Toss lightly with the cubed bread. Chill.
2. Preheat the oven to 350 degrees F.
3. Wrap each chicken breast around ¼ cup stuffing. Bake for 25 to 35 minutes. Slice diagonally. Simmer 2 cups stock and Champagne in a pan.
4. Reduce the cream in another saucepan by ⅛. Stir into the Champagne mixture. Whisk in the cubed butter and cornstarch dissolved in water. Simmer until thickened. Arrange chicken over sauce.

Serves 10

Gathered At The Gables – Then and Now

Maple Cranberry Chicken Breasts

2 teaspoons butter
2 teaspoons prepared garlic
¼ cup all-purpose flour
⅛ teaspoon sea salt
⅛ teaspoon pepper
⅛ teaspoon rosemary leaves
4 boneless, skinless chicken breasts
3 scallions white and light green, chopped
10 mushrooms, sliced
½ cup maple syrup
2 tablespoons apple cider vinegar
2 tablespoons water
¼ cup dried cranberries

1. Melt butter in sauté pan on medium heat. Add garlic.
2. Place flour, salt, pepper and rosemary in a bowl or plastic bag. Coat chicken pieces in flour mixture and brown in pan on both sides. Add green onions and mushrooms to pan.
3. Mix together maple syrup, vinegar and water. Pour over chicken once chicken is browned. Sprinkle cranberries around chicken pieces.
4. Reduce heat to a high simmer for 20 minutes.

Serves 6

Cook's Note: Check chicken frequently to make sure the liquid isn't evaporating too much. Add a little water at a time if it is. It should be a little saucy.

Chicken Tenderloin
with Mustard Sauce

1 pound chicken tenderloins, sliced lengthwise
all-purpose flour
sea salt and pepper
2 tablespoons butter
2 tablespoons oil
⅔ cup dry white wine
⅔ cup chicken broth
3 tablespoons Dijon mustard
1½ teaspoons cornstarch
1½ tablespoons water
½ cup dried cranberries
¼ cup sliced green onions, green part only

1. Lightly toss chicken pieces with flour, shake off excess. Sprinkle lightly with salt and pepper.
2. Heat 1 tablespoon each of the butter and oil in a large skillet. Add half of the chicken. Cook about 2 minutes, turning once, until chicken is golden brown on each side and cooked through. Add more butter and oil, if needed. Remove chicken to a platter; keep warm.
3. Repeat with remaining chicken.
4. Add wine, chicken broth and mustard to skillet, scraping up all browned bits.
5. Combine cornstarch and water in a small bowl or measuring cup.
6. Stir into skillet mixture. Add dried cranberries. Boil 1 or 2 minutes or until sauce thickens.
7. Stir in green onions; cook 1 minute. Pour sauce over chicken and serve.

Serves 8

Blue Ribbon Cranberry Chicken

1 envelope regular onion soup mix
1 (2½ – 3-pounds) broiler-fryer chicken, cut up
1 (16-ounce) can of whole cranberry sauce
1 (8-ounce) bottle of reduced-calorie Russian salad
   dressing with honey (about 1 cup) or regular
   Russian salad dressing
fresh rosemary (optional)
hot cooked rice (optional)

1. In a bowl, combine cranberry sauce, salad dressing and soup mix.
2. Rinse chicken; pat dry with paper towels. Remove and discard skin, if desired. Arrange pieces in one layer in a 13 x 9 x 2-inch baking dish.
3. Pour cranberry mixture over chicken pieces. Cover and chill the chicken mixture in the refrigerator for several hours or overnight.
4. Preheat oven to 300 degrees F. Bake the chicken mixture, uncovered for about 1½ hours, or until the chicken is done, stirring the glaze and spooning over chicken once or twice.
5. Serve the chicken and glaze on a platter with hot, cooked rice, if desired. Garnish the chicken with fresh rosemary.

Serves 4

Eagle River Cranberry Festival Bakeoff

Chicken with
Cranberry-Mustard Sauce

4 large chicken breast halves, skinless, boneless
1 teaspoon onion powder
1 teaspoon dried thyme
sea salt and pepper, to taste
4 tablespoons (½ stick) butter
2 tablespoons all-purpose flour
½ teaspoon dry mustard
1½ cups low-salt chicken broth
¾ cup frozen concentrated cranberry juice
   cocktail, thawed
¼ cup dried cranberries

1. Sprinkle chicken with onion powder, dried thyme, salt and pepper.
2. Melt 2 tablespoons butter in heavy large skillet over medium-high heat. Add chicken and sauté until brown, about 5 minutes per side; transfer to plate.
3. Add remaining butter to skillet and melt. Whisk in flour and mustard; cook 1 minute. Gradually whisk in broth, juice concentrate, and dried cranberries. Boil until sauce thickens enough to coat spoon, about 6 minutes.
4. Return chicken to skillet. Reduce heat to medium low and simmer until chicken is cooked through, about 5 minutes.
5. Season to taste and serve.

Serves 4

Turkey and Cranberry Panini

4 thick slices of Italian bread
2 tablespoons whole-berry cranberry sauce
2 tablespoons mayonnaise
1 chipotle chile canned in adobo sauce,*
  finely chopped
1 cup packed fresh baby spinach leaves
2 slices red onion
8 ounces sliced turkey
2 slices Monterey Jack
3 tablespoons butter or olive oil

1. Stir cranberry sauce, mayonnaise and chipotle in small bowl until well mixed.
2. For each sandwich, spread one side of each slice of bread with cranberry mayonnaise mixture. Place half of the spinach, an onion slice, 4 ounces of turkey and a slice of cheese on bottom half of roll. Place top of roll on sandwich and flatten. Brush both sides of sandwiches with olive oil or butter.
3. Heat sandwiches in panini press according to manufacturer's directions, or heat in a large skillet over medium heat just as you would cook a grilled cheese sandwich. To simulate the panini press, place a heavy pan or skillet on top of the sandwich as it browns in the pan and cook for 10 minutes, turning once or until sandwich is toasted and hot throughout.

Yields: 2 sandwiches

* Cook's Note: Found in the Mexican section of large grocery stores or in specialty Mexican supermarkets.

A cranberry vine takes between three to five years to begin producing. Growers do not need to worry about replanting this perennial plant, because they can survive indefinitely providing they are not damaged.
On Cape Cod, some vines are more than 150 years old.

SIDES

Preserves

Sauces

Vegetables

Dressings

Cranberry Orange Marmalade

2 oranges
1 lemon
2½ cups water
3 cups fresh cranberries
1 (1¾ ounce package) powdered fruit pectin
6½ cups sugar

1. Remove peel from oranges and lemon. Scrape white membrane and cut peel into thin strips.
2. Add peel to 2½ cups water in large saucepan and cook, covered, over low heat 20 minutes.
3. Section oranges and lemon, discard membranes, and cut fruit into small pieces.
4. Add cranberries to peel and simmer 10 minutes, stirring constantly. Stir in pectin and bring to a boil. Stir in sugar; bring to a full rolling boil. Boil hard 1 minute, stirring constantly.
5. Remove from heat and skim foam, if any. Let stand 15 minutes, stirring now and then.
6. Ladle into hot, clean pint jars to within 8-inch of top. Wipe rims and put on lids. Put on screw bands and turn as tightly as possible by hand. Process in boiling waterbath 5 minutes.

Yields: 4 pints

The Boston Globe Cookbook

Cranberry Jam

1 orange
2 cups fresh or frozen cranberries
1 Bartlett pear, peeled and cubed
1 package Certo™ crystals
2 cups white sugar

1. Zest and segment orange, keeping all juice.
2. Place cranberries in a medium saucepan and combine with cranberries, pears and Certo.
3. Bring to a boil.
4. Add sugar and continue to boil while constantly stirring for 2 minutes, then cool.

Yields: 4 cups

Winter Jam

3 cups cranberries, picked over and washed
2 apples, peeled, cored, diced
1 cup water
4 tablespoons lemon juice
1 cup crushed pineapple
2 cups sugar

1. Cook cranberries and apples in water until tender.
2. Add lemon; pineapple and sugar. Mix well. Bring to boil. Reduce heat and boil gently until thick and clear. Skim any foam from top of pan.
3. Pour into sterilized jars and seal.

Yields: 4 to 6 (8 ounce) jars

Green Briar Jam Kitchen Cook Book

Spiced Cranberries

1 cup water
1 ½ cups brown sugar
½ teaspoon ground cinnamon
½ teaspoon ground allspice
½ teaspoon ground cloves
1 pound cranberries, washed

1. Combine all ingredients except cranberries in a heavy saucepan. Bring to a boil; then simmer over low heat for 20 minutes. Add cleaned cranberries.
2. Cook over very low heat for 2 hours, stirring occasionally. Pack immediately into hot, sterilized jars, seal, and process 5 minutes in hot-water bath.
3. The spiced berries may also be kept in covered container in the refrigerator.

Serves 6

The Martha's Vineyard Cookbook

Cranberry Butter

1 ½ cups confectioners sugar
1 cup cranberries, fresh or frozen
¼ (1 stick) pound butter, softened
1 teaspoon lemon juice

1. Combine all ingredients together in a food processor.
2. Process all ingredients with the chopping blade until berries are chopped small.

Yields: 1 cup

Cranberry Apple Butter

3 cups cranberries
2 pounds Golden Delicious apples peeled,
    cored and coarsely chopped
1 cup sugar
½ teaspoon ground cinnamon

1. In a covered four-quart saucepan heat all
   ingredients over high heat until sugar melts and
   mixture boils.
2. Reduce heat to medium and cook covered until
   apples and cranberries are tender—about 20 to 25
   minutes—stirring occasionally.
3. With a potato masher, mash apple mixture until
   almost smooth. If you prefer a smoother texture
   use a food processor. Spoon into serving bowl,
   cover and refrigerate until well chilled—about 3
   hours to 1 week.

Yields: 1 quart

*In 2005, Wisconsin produced over
3.5 million barrels of cranberries
compared to 1.5 million for
Massachusetts. New Jersey, Oregon
and Washington producing another
1.13 million barrels each. In
Massachusetts, production comes
from 14,400 acres compared to
18,000 acres in Wisconsin.*

Cranberry-Pear Sauce

1½ cups cranberry juice cocktail
2 tablespoons cornstarch
1 tablespoon brown sugar
1 teaspoon orange peel, finely shredded
⅛ teaspoon ground cinnamon
2 pears, peeled, cored and chopped

1. Combine cranberry juice, cornstarch, brown sugar, orange peel and ground cinnamon.
2. Cook and stir over medium heat till thickened and bubbly. Cook and stir 2 minutes more.
3. Stir in chopped pears.
4. Refrigerate until ready to use, but not longer than 1 week.

Yields: 2 cups

Cranberry Maple Syrup

¾ cup packed brown sugar
¾ cup water
¼ cup maple syrup
2¼ cups cranberries
2 tablespoons butter

1. In a saucepan combine brown sugar, water and syrup. Stir to dissolve sugar. Heat to boiling; reduce heat.
2. Simmer, uncovered for 5 minutes. Add cranberries; cook until skins pop. Remove from heat.
3. Press mixture through sieve. Stir in butter.
4. Serve warm over pancakes

Yields: 3-4 cups

Cranberry Applesauce

4 pounds apples (use at least 3 different types),
  cut into chunks (don't peel or core)
3 cups cranberries
1 cup unsweetened apple cider
2 (3-inch) strips lemon zest
½ cup sugar
1 teaspoon ground cinnamon

1. In covered pot, simmer apples, berries, cider and
   lemon zest, stirring. Cook ½ hour, until apples are
   very tender.
2. Add sugar and cinnamon. Simmer, covered for 10
   minutes. Discard the zest. Pass mixture through a
   food mill over a bowl.

Yields: 2 quarts

Traditional Cranberry Sauce

2 cups of fresh cranberries
2 tablespoons orange zest
½ teaspoon cinnamon
¼ teaspoon clove or ginger
½ cup of sugar or ⅓ cup honey
⅔ cup of water or orange juice

1. Rinse fresh berries and remove stems. Place
   ingredients in saucepan.
2. Bring to a boil on high heat, boil until all berries
   pop open. Add orange zest, cinnamon, cloves or
   ginger, sugar or honey to taste.
3. Pour into a serving bowl and cool to set.

Yields: 1 pint

Cranberry Vinegar

1 cup fresh or frozen cranberries
2 tablespoons sugar
2 cups distilled white vinegar

1. In a medium saucepan, combine all the ingredients saving a few cranberries to put in the bottle; bring to a boil. Remove from the heat and let stand for 1 hour.
2. Strain through a fine mesh sieve lined with cheesecloth and placed over a bowl.
3. Pour the vinegar into a clean bottle. Add a few berries for color and decoration.
4. Re-seal and store in the refrigerator for up to 1 month.

Yields: 2 cups

In days gone bye, cranberries were poured down steps. The bad ones stayed on the steps because they did not bounce, hence the nickname "bouncing berries". Today each berry has seven chances to bounce over a four-inch barrier. Bounce away!!

Cranberry Salsa

2 cups cranberries
1½ cups orange sections, coarsely chopped
⅓ cup red onion, chopped
⅓ cup fresh orange juice
3 tablespoons sugar
2 tablespoons fresh cilantro, chopped
¼ teaspoon sea salt
1 Jalapeno pepper, seeded and finely chopped

1. Place cranberries in a food processor; pulse 2 to 3 times or until coarsely chopped. Combine cranberries, orange sections, and remaining ingredients in a large bowl, tossing gently to combine.
2. Cover and chill.

Yields: 3 cups

Cranberry Relish

1 unpeeled orange, seeded, cut in quarters
1 cup unpeeled apple, chopped
1 (8-ounce can) juice-pack crushed pineapple
⅓ cup sugar
2 cups fresh cranberries, coarsely ground

1. Grind the orange coarsely in a food processor.
2. Mix with apple, pineapple, sugar and cranberries in a medium bowl.
3. Chill, uncovered, for 8 hours.

Serves 16

Gathered At the Gables – Then and Now

Cranberry Mustard Sauce

¾ cup dry red wine
¾ cup sugar
1 large bay leaf
1 (12-ounce) bag cranberries
1½ tablespoons red wine vinegar
1½ tablespoons dry mustard
sea salt and pepper to taste

1. In a large saucepan, combine the wine, sugar and bay leaf and bring to a boil, stirring to dissolve the sugar.
2. Boil until syrupy, about 9 minutes.
3. Add the cranberries and cook until they begin to break down, about 5 minutes. In a small bowl, whisk the vinegar with the mustard, then whisk the mixture into the cranberries. Season with salt and pepper.
4. Refrigerate and use within one week.

Yields: approximately 2½ cups

Cook's Note – good condiment to use with poultry, ham and duck.

By 1864, a year after Lincoln proclaimed the first national Thanksgiving Day, General Grant ordered a shipment of cranberries so that weary soldiers could celebrate a traditional Thanksgiving properly.

Cran-Apple Squash Boats

2 cups fresh cranberries
4 apples, peeled and chopped
½ cup water
¼ cup sugar
2 teaspoons ginger
½ teaspoon cinnamon
¼ teaspoon allspice
4 Acorn squash
1 tablespoon vegetable oil
1 tablespoon honey

1. Preheat oven to 350 degrees F.
2. Combine the cranberries, apples, water, and sugar in a saucepan. Cook until tender. Strain into a bowl. Add the seasonings.
3. Slice the squash into halves lengthwise, discarding seeds. Arrange in a greased rectangular baking dish; add 1½ inches hot water. Drizzle with the oil and honey. Fill with the fruit sauce.
4. Bake for 20 to 25 minutes or until fork tender.

Serves 8

Gathered At The Gables – Then and Now

Cranberry Maple Squash

3 pounds Butternut Squash, peeled and cubed
2 tablespoons maple syrup
½ teaspoon sea salt
½ cup fresh or frozen cranberries
¼ cup sugar
2 tablespoons maple syrup

1. Preheat oven to 375 degrees F. Spray pan with cooking oil so squash does not stick.
2. In shallow roasting pan, toss squash with 2 tablespoons maple syrup, and salt. Spread in single layer in shallow roasting pan and roast 35 to 40 minutes, turning frequently, until tender and golden. Drain squash before mixing with cranberry mixture.
3. In a small saucepan, combine cranberries, 2 tablespoons sugar and maple syrup. Cook over medium heat until sugar dissolves and coats cranberries. Toss cranberries and their syrup with squash. Serve hot.

Serves 6

Taste and Tales of Massachusetts

Glazed Brussel Sprouts with Dried Cranberries

2½ pounds small Brussels sprouts, trimmed
¼ cup (½ stick) butter
2 tablespoons sugar
½ cup chicken broth
½ cup golden raisins
½ cup dried cranberries, roughly chopped
sea salt & pepper to taste

1. In a medium saucepan over medium-high heat, cook Brussels sprouts for 3 minutes in boiling water until they are partially cooked.
2. Drain and refresh them in ice-cold water, re-drain and set aside.
3. Melt butter in a frying pan over medium-high heat. Add sugar, chicken broth and Brussels sprouts. Cook, tossing regularly until sprouts are tender and the broth is reduced, about 15 to 20 minutes.
4. Stir in raisins and cranberries and cook for an additional 3 minutes. Season with salt and pepper.

Serves 6

Adapted from Big Y® Supermarkets

Green Beans Falmouth

1½ pounds fresh green beans
6 slices bacon, diced
2 tablespoons sugar
2 tablespoons cider vinegar
2 tablespoons water
½ cup green onions, sliced
¾ cup dried cranberries
1 large head iceberg lettuce

1. Tip green beans and cut in 1-inch lengths. Cook covered in boiling salt water for 20 minutes or until crisply tender. Drain and return to saucepan.
2. Sauté bacon until crisp in a small frying pan. Remove and drain on paper toweling; combine with beans.
3. Pour all drippings from pan; then measure 2 tablespoons and return to pan. Stir in sugar, vinegar and green onions. Heat, stirring constantly to boiling. Pour over beans and bacon; toss lightly to mix.
4. Break lettuce into bite-size pieces; layer with bean mixture into a large salad bowl. Toss just before serving.

Serves 6-8

Pearl Onions with Cranberries

1½ pounds pearl onions
2 tablespoons butter
½ cup sugar
2 cups cranberries, fresh or frozen
⅓ cup chicken broth
sea salt & pepper to taste

1. Preheat oven to 400 degrees F.
2. Peel onions and drop in boiling water for 2-3 minutes; drain. Place in cool water.
3. Trim ends of onions, removing outer papery layer and thin transparent layer. Score root end.
4. In a large skillet, cook onions in butter until lightly browned. Stir onions in skillet occasionally to prevent sticking.
5. Add sugar; toss to coat. Add cranberries and seasonings. Add chicken broth and scrape bottom of skillet. Place onion in a non-aluminum baking pan 11x7-inches.
6. Bake for about 30 minutes until onions are soft and glazed.

Serves 8

Taste and Tales of Massachusetts

Wild Rice, Sausage, Almonds and Cranberry Dressing Stuffing

6 cups (½-inch) cubes of day-old French bread
½ cup slivered almonds
¾ pound Italian sausage
2 large onions, chopped
1 teaspoon dried rosemary, crushed
1 teaspoon dried sage leaves, crumbled
1⅓ cups wild rice
4 to 6 cups chicken broth
1 (12-ounce) package fresh cranberries
1 tablespoon melted butter

1. Dry bread cubes in a 350 degrees F oven by spreading on a shallow baking pan and baking for 20 minutes, until lightly browned.
2. Toast almonds by spreading on a cookie sheet and baking in a 350 degrees F oven for 10 minutes, shaking pan occasionally.
3. Sauté sausage, onions, and herbs in a large skillet until onion is tender.
4. In large saucepan, combine wild rice with four cups chicken broth, bring to a boil, cover and lower heat to a simmer. Cook for 45 minutes, stirring occasionally. Drain rice, reserving liquid.
5. In large bowl, combine breadcrumbs, almonds, sausage mixture, wild rice and cranberries; place in a 13x9-inch baking dish. Measure reserved broth and add enough additional broth to make three cups; drizzle over dressing.

6. Cover with foil and bake in a 350° degrees F oven for 40 minutes, until heated through.
7. Uncover, drizzle with melted butter and bake for 10 minutes more.

Serves 8

Adapted from National Pork Board

There are two ways to harvest the little red berry – dry and wet. With the dry method, a mechanical picker with metal teeth combs the berries off their vines. Berries picked by this method supply about 15 percent of the crop. In wet harvesting, the bogs are flooded with water, then worked over by giant "eggbeaters." The berries float to the surface, collected and taken to be made into sauces, jellies or juices, or dried.

Wild Rice, Walnut and Cranberry Dressing

2 tablespoons butter
1 large onion, finely chopped
4 garlic cloves, minced
2 (6-ounce) boxes of wild rice blend
1½ cups toasted walnuts, chopped
½ cup dried cranberries
½ cup fresh parsley, finely chopped.
sea salt and pepper to taste

1. In a large saucepan with a tight-fitting lid, melt butter over medium heat. Sauté onion, stirring occasionally, until soft and golden brown. Add garlic and continue cooking; season with salt and pepper.
2. Add 3 cups of water; bring to a boil. Stir in wild rice blend. Return to a boil and then reduce heat to simmer. Cover and cook over low heat until rice has absorbed all liquid, about 30 minutes. Remove from heat; let stand, covered for 10 minutes.
3 Transfer rice to a large bowl. Stir in walnuts, cranberries and parsley; season again wit salt and pepper. Serve immediately.

Serves 8

Cook's Note: To toast walnuts, spread in a single layer on a rimmed baking sheet. Bake at 350 until golden brown and fragrant, about 10 minutes.

Wild Rice & Dried Fruit Pilaf

2 cups chicken broth
1 cup wild rice
1 tablespoon butter
1 onion, sliced in thin wedges
2 teaspoons brown sugar, firmly packed
¼ cup golden raisins
¼ cup dried cranberries
¼ dried apricots, chopped
1 teaspoon orange zest, grated
1 orange, juice only
¼ teaspoon pepper
2 tablespoons fresh parsley, chopped

1. Combine chicken broth and wild rice in medium saucepan; bring to boil. Reduce heat, cover and simmer 40 minutes or until almost tender.
2. In small saucepan, melt butter over low heat, stir in onion and brown sugar. Cook ten minutes, stirring occasionally, until onion is tender and lightly browned.
3. Add to rice the cooked onions, raisins, cranberries, apricots, orange zest, orange juice and pepper. Cover and simmer ten minutes or until rice is tender and grains have puffed open. Stir in parsley and serve warm.

Serves 6

Notes

Recipe Index

VEGETABLES

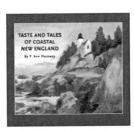

TOP TEN REASONS
to Recommend Cranberries

10. Cranberries contain proanthocyanidins (PACs) and other polyphenols that help to prevent free radical damage.

9. The unusual PACs found in cranberries have a linkage structure that sets them apart from most other fruits and vegetables and is responsible for their anti-adhesion properties.

8. Several studies show that the total antioxidant capacity of the cranberry consistently ranks higher than most other berries and commonly consumed fruits

7. Cranberry PACs help ward off urinary tract infections by preventing E. coli from adhering to the walls of the pladder and multiplying. Instead, the bacteria get flushed out in the urine, reducing the risk of infection.

6. By reducing H. pylori levels in infected subjects, cranberries may help reduce the risk of stomach ulcers. H. pylori is a major risk factor for stomach cancer.

5 Cranberries may have a potential role in lowering the risk of cardiovascular disease by delaying and supressing LDL oxiation.

4. Results from laboratory and animal studies have shown that extracts from cranberries inhibit the growth and proliferation of breast, colon, prostate, lung and esophageal tumor cells.

3. Cranberries are naturally fat-free and have very little sodium.

2. One cup of cranberries has 4 grams of fiber, 65 mg of potassium and 20% of the Daily Value for vitamin C.

1. Available year round, cranberries are easy to incorporate into daily living—dried, fresh, as sauce or in a fruit juice cocktail—and all forms provide beneficial PACs!

Courtesy of the Cranberry Institute
(www.cranberryinstitute.org)